It's Easy to Fake...
Rock Guitar

by Joe Bennett

Exclusive Distributors:
Music Sales Corporation
257 Park Avenue South, New York, NY10010, USA.
Music Sales Limited
8/9 Frith Street, London W1D 3JB, England.
Music Sales Pty Limited
120 Rothschild Avenue, Rosebery, NSW 2018, Australia.

Order No. AM 973764
ISBN 0.8256.1927.0
This book © Copyright 2002 Amsco Publications

Written by Joe Bennett.
Edited by Sorcha Armstrong.
Musical examples by Richard Barrett.
Music engraving by Digital Music Art.

Book design by Phil Gambrill.
Cover design by Michael Bell Design.
Illustrations by Andy Hammond.

All text photographs courtesy of
London Features International
except: Jimi Hendrix (page 18) and
Scotty Moore (page 26) - Redferns;
Spinal Tap (page 29) - The Kobal Collection.
Specialist guitar pictures (pages 89-93)
supplied courtesy of Balafon Books.

Printed in the United States of America by
Vicks Lithograph and Printing Corporation

www.musicsales.com

It's Easy to Fake...
Rock Guitar

by Joe Bennett

Amsco Publications
London / New York / Paris / Sydney / Copenhagen / Madrid / Tokyo

Introduction 7
The History of Rock 8
The Players...

Music and TAB Guide 30
The Music...

Music Shop Classic 80
Music Shop Riffs 84
Amps 86
Guitars...

Rock Lyrics 94
Outro 96

Chuck Berry: the Godfather of rock

Introduction

Whatever reasons a guitarist has for picking up an electric guitar, you can bet a truckload of leather jackets that rock was involved in some way or another. It's all very well to learn beautiful classical solo pieces to perform in front of your grandparents, or acoustic folk numbers to play at the local barn dance, but deep down, most players have a burning desire to get up on stage and yell at the audience "are you ready to rawwwwk?!".

Unfortunately, a great deal of rock guitar playing takes years — sometimes decades — of practice. To become truly proficient, you may have to learn (ugh!) scales and (yuck!) arpeggios and possibly even (aaaaargh!) how to read music. Luckily, help is at hand. *It's Easy to Fake Rock Guitar* explains how, with the right information, equipment, clothes, name-dropping skills and attitude, you can become an expert in all the local customs of 'planet rock'. Learn what to say and when to say it. Find out which players you can mention at a gig without ridicule. And play the riffs and licks that will have other musicians worshipping at your feet.

For example

Guitarists naturally have a tendency to judge each other by technical skill. The rock bluffer need show no fear, even when confronted with the most well-practiced virtuoso. Any rival who can play stunning sweep-picking arpeggios at 10 notes per second can be dismissed as 'passé', 'retro', or 'a heavy metal dinosaur'. Players who achieve super-accurate scalic runs should be accused of 'having no feel' or 'missing the point'.

Of course, if you get stuck in a situation when your playing really is on the line, we've helpfully supplied just a smattering of impressive musical examples which you can throw into solos whenever you think the audience need reminding of your complete mastery of the instrument.

It's Easy to Fake Rock Guitar gives you an unfair advantage over other guitarists. It's an immoral, cheating, deceitful, unethical and deceptive way of improving your guitar playing. So now all you need to do is go out and buy up all the other copies so that no-one else gets their hands on them...

The History of Rock or
'Who to name-drop, and when'

A true rock god will, when interviewed, make frequent reference to early blues. You know the kind of thing; "sure, we're into thrash-industrial-speed-punk-techno-metal these days, but sooner or later we're gonna go back to our roots and do an album of Robert Johnson covers." This is a perfectly valid bluffer's tactic, but doesn't really represent the truth in musical terms.

Origins

Rock music as we now know it is largely derived from R&B, so when you're name-checking influences the best era to start looking is the 1950s. Without a doubt the most influential guitar player from this era was **Chuck Berry**. Every rock player of the last four decades owes something to him, and many of the techniques we take for granted first appeared on his recordings.

Aerosmith wouldn't be using palm-muted downstrokes were it not for Chuck. **The Sex Pistols** wouldn't have played their driving, 8-to-the-bar chord parts without the influence of the great man. And The Rolling Stones' **Keith Richards** alleges he would never have picked up the guitar in the first place if he hadn't heard those early Berry singles on Chess records.

Mostly, you'll fake your way through any 'rock roots' conversation just by demonstrating your detailed knowledge about Chuck (see page 14), but it's also useful to have a sentence or two about some of his contemporaries, even though they will generally win you less cool points.

Bluffer's rule #1: Whatever style you play, **Chuck Berry** is your biggest influence.

Eddie Cochran (perhaps the first rock guitar hero) and **Duane Eddy** (first rock guitar instrumentalist) are both worth a mention. Even **Hank Marvin** (not a name you'd normally bring up in a roomful of hairy rockers) was an innovator — he was the first Strat player in the UK, and also pioneered whammy-bar string bends.

Despite the fact that many classic rock acts started in the early '60s (**The Stones**, **The Kinks** and **The Who** to name but three), most of the choice name-drops occur in the later part of the decade. If you know your **Hendrix**, early **Pink Floyd**, **Jefferson Airplane** and **Cream**, you'll find that nine times out of ten you won't even have to go any further back than this.

The 1970s

This is by far the easiest decade to discuss for the would-be rock guru, because it's very difficult to put a wrong foot forward. No-one will argue against your assertions of the influence of Jimmy Page on your playing. Early Thin Lizzy and Van Halen recordings still command maximum credibility among rock veterans.

Bluffer's rule # 2:
If you *have* to name-drop a 1970s HM act...

Even artists who were considered extremely lame just a few years ago (**Slade, Marc Bolan, Kiss, Sweet**) can, if you fake confidently enough, be used to demonstrate your unsurpassed appreciation of kitsch and irony in a rock context (hint: this is fairly advanced faking, and should only be attempted after you've spent some time on entry-level concoctions).

Of course, it's not possible to ignore the fact that around this time, heavy metal was starting to claw its Satanic way into the album charts. It can be difficult to divorce the players from the paraphernalia (skulls, crucifixes, Viking helmets, rune-clad mystic symbols etc) so if you *have* to name-drop a 1970s HM act, at least try to choose one whose clothes you'd be happy to be seen in yourself.

... at least try to choose one whose clothes you'd be happy to be seen in yourself.

The 1980s

During this period, guitar sounds, stadium crowds, and hairstyles all got bigger at the same rate. Many bands who first recorded in the 1970s had continued success (**Queen, AC/DC, Dire Straits, ZZ Top**). However, the development of the synthesizer eventually led to the birth of rock music's all-too-legitimate offspring — the Adult Oriented Rock band.

Bluffer's rule #3: Don't admit to owning any albums by **REO Speedwagon**.

Whatever your personal view of AOR acts like **REO Speedwagon**, **Journey** and **Foreigner**, it is faking suicide to even mention one of their songs, let alone be caught in possession of an album. The other phenomenon that appeared during this decade was the fretboard tapping virtuoso. Just a few years after **Van Halen**'s first album, the likes of **Vinnie Moore, Joe Satriani, Jennifer Batten, Steve Vai** and **Paul Gilbert** were wowing the guitar-playing community with their instrumental technique.

Warning: it's extremely difficult to navigate your way through a conversation about these players with your status intact. Some are safe to mention and will guarantee admiring glances etc, others will earn you promises that you'll never work again in this town... that's if you don't have your fingers broken for alluding to them in the first place.

To give an example, **Yngwie Malmsteen** and **Steve Vai** are both very fine players (even having played in the same band at different times), yet Vai's name is positively celestial to guitarists, whereas citing Malmsteen as an influence will (at best) result in you being firmly directed to the nearest exit. There's no real rule of thumb to help you here — you'll just need to learn which players are 'safe ground'.

Bluffer's rule #4: Learn your shredders.

The 1990s

In recent years, advanced guitar techniques have, to some extent, taken a back seat. This is great news for a rock charlatan like oneself, because it's now possible to look cool with considerably less time spent in the practice-room.

Bluffer's rule #5: You don't have to practice too hard...

Kurt Cobain and **Noel Gallagher**, for example, are guitar heroes to millions, and yet neither of them are particularly adept players. Concentrating too much on the subject of technique can actually damage your reputation in some circles; the worst criticism you can make of another player is to say "he's good, but *so* 'eighties'." Admittedly, there are still some advanced players on the current scene — **Kim Thayill** of Soundgarden, The Chilis' **Dave Navarro**, Ex-Living Colour guitarist **Vernon Reid** etc, but in the mainstream the big rock guitar heroes (**Eric Clapton**, **Jimi Hendrix**, **Mark Knopfler**) have hardly changed in the last 20 years.

Bluff your way through the 21st century

So the rock bluffers of the 21st century need to be good players - but not too good. If you're technique's already pretty hot, try toning down the quality of your playing by adding so much distortion that no-one can hear it properly.

If you're not an advanced player, you'll still need a few flash licks now and again so you can demonstrate to the audience that your incessant strumming of one chord is actually down to a sense of musical restraint rather than a lack of ideas. Eventually, of course, the pendulum will swing back and technique will reign supreme again. But by that time you'll have had more time to practice, won't you?

Bluffer's rule #6: ... but if you get *really* good, make sure no-one can decipher what you're playing.

Jeff Beck: a true rock pioneer and still one of the most innovative players around

The Players

Bite-size bios

Rock purists will consider it blasphemy to have a player's entire life summarized in two pages, but in reality, you can fake your way through with a surprisingly small amount of knowledge. In this chapter you'll find an instant guide to six top rock guitarists.

Remember that these aren't necessarily the most important or famous players — we haven't included **Ritchie Blackmore** or **Mark Knopfler**, for example — but they are the names which crop up most frequently in rock gig-speak. Obviously **Jimi Hendrix** (possibly the most discussed guitarist of all time) appears here, but note that he also appears in another book in this series — *It's Easy to Fake Blues Guitar.*

For each artist, I've included some basic **biographical information**, notes on **playing style**, plus (most importantly) which **techniques** you should steal in order to facilitate your faking career. Of course, you have to know the **gear** they used - equipment aficinados are everywhere and could pounce at any time.

To save you from having to wade through a truckload of albums, I've also picked out one **essential album** for you to mention (not necessarily the best-known — it can sometimes pay dividends to fake your way by showing you listen to the obscure stuff). If you're actually asked to prove that you've heard the artist, you'd be stuck without the quick and easy **'finest moment'** reference.

Finally, it's always useful to have a few oven-ready opinions up your sleeve. For each player, I've included an 'instant opinion' (usually ambiguous enough to cover all situations) and an 'acceptable criticism'. If you're cool enough to intelligently criticize one of the greats, your status as a blackbelt bluffer is assured.

Chuck Berry

HISTORY AND BACKGROUND:

Born 18th October 1931 *or* 15th January 1926. Like many aspects of Chuck's shady past, his birthdate is still the subject of controversy (he's had various brushes with the law, including armed robbery and 'transporting a minor across a state line for immoral purposes'). 1955 single 'Maybelline' was an instant R&B hit — perhaps the first ever rock recording. Early recordings ('Around and Around', 'Come On', 'Rock and Roll Music', 'Roll Over Beethoven') were heavily covered by British acts — **Rolling Stones, Beatles, Animals, Yardbirds**. Famously eccentric live performer. As well as his trademark 'duckwalk', (see page 6) Chuck is known for always insisting on being paid cash for every performance. He doesn't travel with a band, preferring to hire and fire players local to the venue, and expecting them to learn his entire repertoire before the gig.

PLAYING STYLE:

Pick downstrokes, 8-to-the-bar. Double-stops (two strings played together) using first finger flattened over the first two strings, or over the second and third. Occasional lead lines harmonized in thirds. Semi-distorted tone. Almost always plays solos in minor pentatonic box shape.

TECHNIQUES TO STEAL:

Double-stops are great for making solos sound energetic and exciting, and best of all they're even easier to play than single-note lines. The duckwalk should be mastered by every guitar player because it's such an essential bit of showmanship — simply put all your weight on one leg and bend it, then kick the other heel into the floor as you hop along (while playing 8-to-the-bar downstrokes). Not as difficult it sounds.

GEAR:

Gibson semi-hollow bodies, mainly cherry red ES-335. Often uses Fender combos, but doesn't worry much about amp types 'so long as it works'.

BLUFFER'S ALBUM:

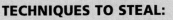

Any compilation 1955-95, but you should also buy a few vinyl singles, regardless of whether you have the equipment to play them. Chess label recordings are still available in second-hand record shops, and if you can get an ex-jukebox one with the center removed, so much the better.

FINEST MOMENT:

The intro from his classic 'Johnny B Goode' (which is almost identical to many others, including 'Roll Over Beethoven' and 'Bye Bye Johnny') or possibly the main riff from later hit 'No Particular Place To Go' (which is the same song, basically, as another hit 'School Days').

INSTANT OPINION:

"The Godfather of Rock 'n' Roll — he's my biggest influence."

ACCEPTABLE CRITICISM:

Didn't break any new ground after about 1960.

Jeff Beck

HISTORY AND BACKGROUND:

Born 24th June 1944. First big break came when he replaced **Clapton** in the Yardbirds (1965). Formed his own self-titled group the following year. First (pop) hit 'Hi Ho Silver Lining' was his biggest single, and inspired some players to experiment with twin lead lines (so he is partly to blame for the existence of **Iron Maiden**).

Never worked consistently with a vocalist, despite sessions or albums with **Donovan**, **Rod Stewart**, **Tina Turner**, **Kate Bush**, **Brian May**, **Jon Bon Jovi** and **Robert Plant**. Two jazz-rock albums mid '70s — *Blow By Blow* and *Wired*. Current output is roughly one or two albums per decade. Very rarely gives interviews, and spends much of his time restoring classic American cars.

PLAYING STYLE:

In a word — stunning. One of the true masters of the electric guitar. Unreal string bends, whammy-bar harmonics, trills, tapping, country-picking. Usually plays with fingers. Despite the flash stuff, though, he's always willing to play more laid-back lead if the song demands it.

TECHNIQUES TO STEAL:

The most interesting is probably whammy-bar harmonics. Hit an open harmonic (say, 5th or 7th fret) and practice bending that one note around using the bar to create melody. It's difficult but the effect is worth it in audience-wowing terms.

GEAR:

Started on Teles, Strats and Les Pauls, but now synonymous with the Strat. Marshall amps.

BLUFFER'S ALBUM:

Jeff Beck's Guitar Shop (1989) is one of his most accessible, while still showing off that technique. But for true credibility points you should own the largely dance-inspired *Who Else* (1999).

FINEST MOMENT:

'Where Were You' from *Jeff Beck's Guitar Shop* features a typical Beck-ism; although it uses lots of repetition, he never plays the same phrase twice with the same tone, using the pickup selector or his picking technique to modify the sound.

INSTANT OPINION:

"Check out the new stuff — he's still one of the most innovative players around."

ACCEPTABLE CRITICISM:

Doesn't release enough material to keep the fans happy.

Jimi Hendrix

HISTORY AND BACKGROUND:

Born 27th November 1942. Allegedly had his name changed by his father from Johnny Allen Hendrix to James Marshall Hendrix. Influenced by **BB King** and **Muddy Waters**, among others. Worked with various soul/R&B acts, including **Little Richard**, **Curtis Knight**, **Ike Turner**, until he was 'discovered' by Animals' bassist **Chas Chandler**, who brought him over to the UK.

The 'Jimi Hendrix Experience' was formed in 1966 with bass player **Noel Redding** and drummer **Mitch Mitchell**. Early hits eventually led to discovery by US audiences. Notable live gigs included Monterey Pop Festival, Woodstock and the Isle of Wight Festival (the latter two occurred after Redding left in 1969). Died in his sleep, choking on his own vomit, on 18th September 1970.

PLAYING STYLE: Pyrotechnic is the word. Outrageous swooping bends, whammy bar dives, controlled (and uncontrolled) feedback, all played Very Loud Indeed. His more laid-back material features subtle grace notes using hammer-ons, and distortion dynamics controlled by the pick. Made great use of the minor pentatonic scale, but solos and riffs also featured major pentatonic, Mixolydian and natural minor scales. Some techniques (e.g. thumb used to fret bass strings) rely on the fact that he had very large hands.

TECHNIQUES TO STEAL: Any of the crowd-pleasing flash techniques (e.g. playing guitar behind your head, setting guitar on fire, lewd behavior with whammy bar etc) are viewed as sacrilegious by most aficionados, so use these with care. However, any technical tricks are up for grabs — try playing trills while moving the whammy bar; moving the wah-wah while playing rapid lead licks; muted 'unpitched' chords used as a percussive effect...).

GEAR: Usually played a right-handed Strat strung left-handed and hung upside-down, through Marshall amps. Also used a variety of stompboxes, modified by English FX guru Roger Mayer. (Name drop opportunity here!)

BLUFFER'S ALBUM: Start with the 1967 Experience album *Axis: Bold As Love*, but eventually you've really got to buy them all (but stay away from early-60s archive re-releases — Jimi was rarely more than a rhythm-playing session man on these recordings).

FINEST MOMENT: Musically, it's probably his cover of Dylan's 'All Along The Watchtower' (exceptional control of bends, consummate tone, beautiful phrasing). However, bluffers would do well to acquaint themselves with his legendary 'Star Spangled Banner' live recording, which uses the guitar to emulate rockets firing, bombs dropping etc. It sounds utterly awful, but of course you must never be seen to admit this.

INSTANT OPINION:
"God came to Earth and walked among us for a few short years."

ACCEPTABLE CRITICISM: Possibly, just possibly, you might tentatively suggest that the guitar could just maybe have been slightly out of tune during 'The Star Spangled Banner'?... (HOW DARE YOU MOCK THE MASTER — GET BACK UNDER WHATEVER ROCK YOU CRAWLED OUT FROM, YOU REVOLTING PIECE OF WORTHLESS SLIME etc).

Brian May

HISTORY AND BACKGROUND:
Born 19th July 1947. Worked in a college band called Smile with drummer **Roger Taylor**, before forming Queen in 1971 with singer **Freddie Mercury** and bassist **John Deacon**. His early influences as a player were originally the **Everly Brothers** and the **Shadows**, but like many rock guitarists he soon learned to fake his way through by namechecking **Chuck Berry** and **Bo Diddley**.

Queen's 25-year career needs little documentation (at the time of writing there are rumors of a reunion with the three remaining members). But Brian's also been an active solo performer both during and after Queen — his 1984 *Starfleet Project* was recorded with **Eddie Van Halen**; he's also done various guest spots and sessions, plus two solo albums.

PLAYING STYLE: Famous for multi-layered harmony guitar parts. These are more intricate than many players first think; often several harmonized lines work against each other. Uses very light strings and picks delicately. Adds whammy bar vibrato to chords.

TECHNIQUES TO STEAL: The harmony thing is pretty tough to copy — even Brian had to use a long delay to duplicate the sound when playing live. Many multi-FX units have harmonizers on-board, but don't attempt to use one of these unless you really know you're music theory. The results can be truly painful. Try using the whammy bar as a subtle addition to your vibrato, rather than always using it for mad dive-bombing antics.

GEAR: Any rock bluffer should know how to identify The Three Eras Of Brian from pictures and album covers. If he's shown with long curly hair, playing a red home-made guitar through a Vox AC30, it dates from the mid-1970s; long curly hair, red home-made guitar and Vox AC30, and it's from the 1980s. If you see him these days, though, it'll be with long curly hair, a red home-made guitar and a Vox AC30.

BLUFFER'S ALBUM: Queen's *A Night at the Opera* is standard issue for any rock music fan, though there's enough water under the bridge now for you to get away with owning the outrageously overblown but guitaristically impressive 1974 album *Queen II*.

FINEST MOMENT: The 'chiming' layered solo from 'Killer Queen' (from the album *Sheer Heart Attack*) is one of Brian's faves, and most fans agree. However, it's impossible for one player to duplicate on their own, so if you're looking for ideas to steal, try the long delay-based 'Brighton Rock' from the same album.

INSTANT OPINION: "Don't buy that Brian May signature guitar — the sound isn't just about his gear, you know — it's in the way he plays."

ACCEPTABLE CRITICISM: Solo material has tended towards bland compared to more adventurous guitar work with Queen.

Edward Van Halen

HISTORY AND BACKGROUND:

Born 26th January 1957. Dutch in origin. Learned drums originally (brother Alex played guitar) but swapped instruments with him before forming Van Halen in 1974. First album *Van Halen* in 1978 was (perhaps!) the first to feature picking-hand fretboard tapping, although this is one of the great bluffers' debates of rock guitar. It appeared briefly on Queen's *It's Late* a year previously, and was allegedly used by **ZZ Top** even earlier (although no-one seems to be able to identify on which track).

Whether or not he was technically the first to tap, EVH still deserves his status as one of the most influential electric guitarists of all time. Has confessed that he doesn't listen to music much these days, as shown by the fact that his material has hardly developed in the last decade or so. Members of the band have publicly apologized for the poor quality of the 1998 album *Van Halen III*.

Note: the initiated now refer to him as 'Edward', rather than 'Eddie' Van Halen. Like Dave 'David' Gilmour, he's gone back to the full version of his name for what we can only assume are reasons of musical maturity.

PLAYING STYLE:

Tapping, harmonics and combinations of same, using distorted and delayed sound, plus flangers, phasers etc as appropriate. Solos are not always just speed-based — he plays some fine melodic material too, especially on the early albums.

TECHNIQUES TO STEAL:

Try to avoid basing your whole style on tapping, but as with all of the show-off techniques, it is worth learning a few basic examples to throw into solos now and again. The Van Halen guitar sound (bridge humbucker through distortion pedal and valve amp with medium-length delay added) was a blueprint used by rock players for years afterwards.

GEAR:

Originally, he used a single-pickup hybrid guitar made from spare parts with an old-style Fender floating bridge, into a Marshall stack. More recently, Ernie Ball and Peavey have made signature models for him. He now uses his own signature Peavey 5150 amp.

BLUFFER'S ALBUM:

Without question, the band's debut is the one to own, but you might also want to be seen with some of their other material from the same era with **Dave Lee Roth** on vocals. The mid-80s Sammy Hagar stuff is scoffed at by many for its production sheen.

FINEST MOMENT:

The instrumental 'Eruption' from *Van Halen* is responsible for some of the greatest aural pain ever to be visited upon the ears of guitar shop assistants, but when you listen to the man himself play it, you can see what all the fuss was about.

INSTANT OPINION:

"Combining melodic playing with tapping — he was the first and still the best."

ACCEPTABLE CRITICISM:

Should get out more and listen to some new music.

Steve Vai

HISTORY AND BACKGROUND:

Born 6th June 1960. First big break came when he worked as a transcriber and then guitar player for the infamously-meticulous **Frank Zappa**. During the 1980s he went on to replace **Yngwie Malmsteen** in flash-metal band **Alcatrazz**, then worked with **Dave Lee Roth** (who had recently quit **Van Halen**).

Solo album *Flex-able* was followed by a stint with **Whitesnake**, with various solo recordings since, all exploring the arty side of virtuoso rock. The man's studio and practice techniques are unconventional, to say the least. He's into meditation, fasting, and using recordings of animals on backing tracks.

PLAYING STYLE:

Whether or not you're into flashy guitar playing, you have to admit that Steve is possibly the world's most technically accomplished rock guitarist. He uses all the techniques popularized by **Van Halen** (whammy bar dives, tapping, pinched/natural/artificial harmonics) and many others besides (multi-layered harmonics in harmony, bar-flicking or 'gargling', weird tunings on six- and seven-string guitars).

TECHNIQUES TO STEAL:

Start with gaining as much pitch control over harmonics as you can, then work on your whammy technique, then be prepared to give up your job and go and live in a rehearsal room for 10 years or so — that's the only way you're going to steal from Steve...

GEAR:

Ibanez Jem and 7-string Universe guitars, designed by Steve (see page 93). Amps mainly Marshall and Soldanos, though he's currently endorsing Carvins.

BLUFFER'S ALBUM:

If you can stand the sexist lyrics, massive 80s-rock production and sparkly keyboard sounds, the guitar playing on Whitesnake's 'Slip of the Tongue' is wonderful. However, if you do buy this album, keep it in a brown paper bag under the bed in case anyone finds out. Vai recordings suitable for the CD rack include *Passion and Warfare* and *Flex-able*, plus any early 1980s Zappa albums.

FINEST MOMENT:

For pure showmanship, watch the movie 'Crossroads' — Steve plays a 'gunslinger' guitar-player character who takes part in a musical duel at the end of the film. For faking purposes, though, you're better off extolling the virtues of one of the solo album tracks — For the Love of God (from *Passion and Warfare*) is a good starting point.

INSTANT OPINION:

"Sure, technically he's pretty good, but he can't play with the feel of Kurt Cobain" (almost certainly untrue, but like all good bluffs, it makes you look knowledgeable, starts an argument, and can't be settled one way or the other).

ACCEPTABLE CRITICISM:

Fashion only, I'm afraid, but there's a wealth of scope there — blue hair (including back-combing), distressed jeans, spandex pants, lace cardigans...

!!?#

Emergency backup bluffs

Here are some bluffing basics on a further six players, just in case you need additional reference to prove your depth of knowledge.

1. Scotty Moore

The most famous of **Elvis Presley**'s guitarists. Was working as a session player at Sun Studios in the early 1950s, before teaming up with **The King** in 1954. Used Gibson archtops (including L-5s and Super 400s). He's responsible for many of the rockabilly double-stopped licks that we know and love today. If anyone plays a rock 'n' roll lick that doesn't sound like **Chuck Berry**, simply describe it as "very Scotty Moore" for instant respect from those in the know.

2. Jimmy Page

Like, you need any information about the man who played 'Stairway to Heaven', right? Well, we should thank Jim for a lot more than merely adding to the guitar shop repertoire. Check out Led Zep's work and you'll hear open acoustic tunings, time signature tricks, and modal improvisations, plus a range of influences from English folk to Indian classical music.

Most famously played sunburst Gibson Les Pauls, but also had several Telecasters and of course the 6/12-string double-necked ES1275 (pictured). Generally he plays electric through a Marshall stack. What else?!

3. Joe Satriani

Probably the biggest guitar hero of the late 1980s. His popularity's taken a bit of a dip lately, partly due to a less-than-great album in 1996, partly due to a lack of commercial interest in instrumental rock generally.

He knows the instrument inside out, though, and his tracks, despite featuring more than a dash of flash, actually have *good melodies*. Ibanez player, mainly through Marshalls. The 'Satch' sound is a very warm, thick, midrange-heavy tone, with compression and delay. Also notable for teaching **Steve Vai** and Metallica's **Kirk Hammett**.

4. Kurt Cobain

When you consider that your average street-corner session player or pub rock musician is likely to be a technically better guitarist than Kurt, it might seem unfair that he's featured on the same page as, er, **Page**, but there's a good reason for it. His aggressive guitar style and Nirvana's sparse sound were defining factors in the development of rock music in the 1990s. Plus, of course, with his self-imposed martyrdom back in 1994, he's become one of the most imitated guitar players of the decade.

Generally played bar chords on the bass strings, using a variety of dropped tunings (with the whole guitar sometimes dropped as much as three whole steps). Used trademark Fender 'Jag-stang' — a cross between the Mustang and Jaguar models.

5. John Squire

Contemporary Indie-rock icon. First came to our attention in 1989 on the **Stone Roses**' debut album. Impersonated **Jimmy Page** outrageously on their next recording, 'Second Coming'. Technically, he's not an especially interesting player (usual pentatonics and bar chords) but much-discussed due to the way he uses the guitar as part of the mix, often layering several different guitars, amps, tones, and tunings to create the overall effect.

Played a Gretsch Country Gent and Fender Jaguar with **the Roses** — currently favours Les Pauls. Bizarrely, you'll find it difficult to criticise his technique in a bluffing environment — everything he does seems to be sacred, despite the fact that he's only done three albums in 13 years.

6. Noel Gallagher

Controversial Britrock player, and possibly the most successful rock bluffer of all time. Has continued to play the same six or seven chords and the same two pentatonic scale shapes throughout his recording career, and consistently has chart success, despite refusal to attempt anything new on the guitar. Depending on whether or not you like Oasis, you can choose to fake either side of the technique debate — if you're a fan, then anyone who criticizes Noel's playing 'just doesn't get it'; if you're not, simply learn three or four Oasis solos note-for-note, and point out to your opponent how similar they are.

Noel plays a 1970 Epiphone Casino almost exclusively, although there's a current signature model you can buy. He's loved and hated by the guitar world — on the one hand, he's responsible for tens of thousands of young people getting into the guitar; on the other, he made them think it sounds OK to thrash away at an open C chord through a wall of distortion.

Spinal Tap
"How much more clichéd can this be..."

In 1980 film director Marti Di Bergi made this classic documentary, or if you will, rockumentary, about an English rock band on their comeback tour of the US. It's become the most quoted movie of all time among rock musicians, and as such the bluffer should know every word of the script by heart.

However, if you've never seen it, here are the most common 'Tap' references you'll hear at gigs, together with the required response.

Situation	Tap reference	Your response
Guitarist has very loud amp — refers to the band's modified Marshalls whose controls go up to 11	"It goes up to eleven"	"That's, like, one louder"
Drummer is late for the gig — refers to Tap drummers who commonly die under mysterious circumstances	"He's probably dead"	"..in a bizarre gardening accident..."
The band hasn't rehearsed, or a key member hasn't turned up — refers to Tap gig shortly after Nigel's resignation	"There's nothing for it"	"we'll have to play Jazz Oddyssey"
Somebody comments on your guitar — refers to interview between Marty and Nigel	"I'll just take a look..."	"Don't even look at it. Don't even point"
Band, stage set, album, guitar or amp is colored black — refers to all-black cover for Tap's 'Smell the Glove' album	"How much more black can this be?"	"None. None... more black"

It's Easy to Fake...
Music and TAB Guide

Most guitar players can't read music. There. We've said it. So you can stop feeling guilty about it and get on with the serious business of pretending that you can. On these two pages you'll find tab and treble clef notation for all of the techniques featured in this book, along with tips on how to play them.

HOW TO READ TREBLE CLEF: The note on the bottom line of the treble clef is middle E — that is, it's the E which is found on the 2nd fret of the D string. The top line is F (1st fret, high E string).

Guitar notes that are lower or higher than this range are notated using 'leger lines' — these are extra staff lines drawn above or below the main clef.

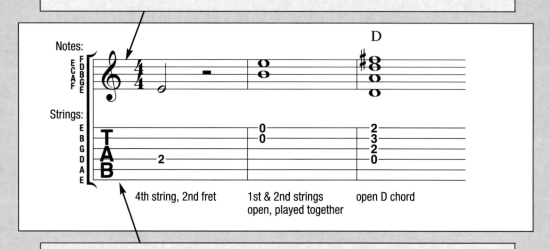

4th string, 2nd fret   1st & 2nd strings open, played together   open D chord

HOW TO READ TAB: The six lines represent the strings – the thickest (lowest) string is on the bottom. The number shows the fret.

HOW TO READ CHORD PARTS: The chord names are written above, and sometimes the musical rhythm of the part is notated underneath.

If no rhythm is given, or you see several even 'slashes' in a bar, then normally you should make up your own rhythm pattern. If you see two chords in a bar, it's normally assumed that they're played for two beats each.

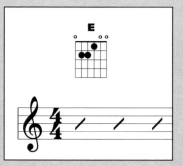

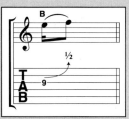

HALF-STEP BEND:
Play the note with the picking hand then bend it up a half step (so it reaches the pitch of the note on the next fret).

WHOLE-STEP BEND:
Duh! Just bend it further!

GRACE NOTE BEND:
The only difference with these is that you start bending as soon as you've picked the note. You should hardly hear the first note.

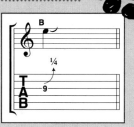

QUARTER-STEP BEND:
Just bend the string a little — don't go as far as a half step. Quarter-step is used to mean any bend that's less than a half step.

BEND AND RELEASE:
Play the note, bend it up, let it back down again.

PRE-BEND:
Bend the note up before you play it.

PRE-BEND AND RELEASE: Bend the note up, then play it, then release the bend while the note rings on.

VIBRATO:
Move the string up and down by rapidly bending and releasing it by a small amount.

HAMMER-ON:
Pick one note, then sound the higher note by fretting it without re-picking. Hammer-ons are always ascending in pitch.

PULL-OFF: Get both fingers into the positions shown in the tab, then pick the higher note. While it rings on, pull the finger off the string to sound the lower note.

SLIDE/GLISS:
While the note is sounding, slide the fretting finger up or down to the position shown in the tab.

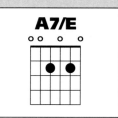

SLIDE/GLISS AND RESTRIKE:
As before, but this time repick the second note after you've finishing sliding.

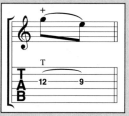

TAPPING: Fret the note using the picking hand by tapping onto the position shown. Usually followed by a pull-off.

PALM MUTING:
Rest the picking hand on the strings very near to the bridge. This partially mutes the notes — the technique is used a lot in blues and rock rhythm playing.

A7/E

SLASH CHORDS:
Many players get confused when they see chord notation like this for the first time. Do not fear — it's simple. The letter name before the slash is the chord you play. The one after the slash is the bass note. Faking tip — if you find it too difficult to play a particular bass note at the same time as the chord, try ignoring it and just playing the chord, then get a bassist or keyboard player to supply the bottom end.

Jimmy Page: stairway to technical mastery

Rhythm Patterns or
'He doesn't want to make it cry or sing'

If you have to fake your way through a whole rock gig, you'll need to convince everyone in the band that you know your 'rock chops', so it's vital that you can play some basic accompaniment styles.

In this section you'll find 10 rhythm and picking patterns, in progressive order of difficulty, that rock guitarists use when playing in a band context behind a singer or lead player.

Rhythm Tips

- Almost every rock player uses a pick rather than fingers for rhythm work. And if you're playing in 4/4 time, you should generally favor downstrokes rather than upstrokes.
- **Rest the picking-hand palm gently on the strings near the bridge to create palm-mutes, then use 8-to-the-bar downstrokes with the pick. This is essential for heavier rock styles.**
- Generally, avoid open major chords like G, C, D etc — they don't sound as good as 'power chords' (see page 68).
- **There's a common misconception that the more distortion you use, the heavier it will sound. This is rarely true, because if you bury the whole mix in distortion, the attack of the chord is lost, so the whole mix doesn't 'rock'.**
- Don't strum all 6 strings, all the time. Most rock rhythm parts only use the bass strings.
- **Experiment with tunings for a heavier sound. Try dropping the bass string down to D, or tuning the whole guitar a half-step lower.**
- Don't use lots of reverb on rhythm parts — it turns the whole sound into a mushy mess.
- **There is no such thing as a tuning that's 'close enough for rock and roll'. If your guitar's out of tune, your rhythm playing will *always* sound wrong. Get an electronic tuner and use it!**
- Use accents. Why should every chord in your rhythm pattern be played at the same volume?
- **Be disciplined. Don't let your concentration wander even if what you're playing is really simple — a good rhythm part often features very little variation.**

'Musical Paranoia'

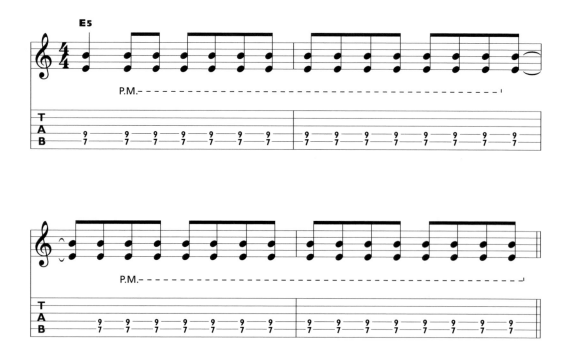

This rhythmic idea owes much of its rock character to the palm muted effect which features throughout, broken up only by ringing chord stabs which can played at different times to vary the accents.

Even on acoustic guitar this can still sound pretty menacing.

'Let There Be Rhythm'

Taking a similar approach to the previous one, this example lends itself to faster tempos. You will hear this kind of rhythm in use on **AC/DC**'s 'Let There Be Rock', among others.

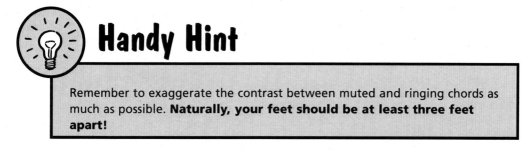

Handy Hint

Remember to exaggerate the contrast between muted and ringing chords as much as possible. **Naturally, your feet should be at least three feet apart!**

'No Latin Quarter'

Highlighting the contrast between muted/ringing notes by playing them in different octaves, this example would be right at home driving along an early 80s style Heavy Rock/Metal track.

Ironically, the rhythm has an almost Latin American quality. However, with the correct (i.e. extreme) volume, distortion and posturing, you can be sure *nobody* will be wuss enough to attempt the cha-cha...

'Skipping Scallies'

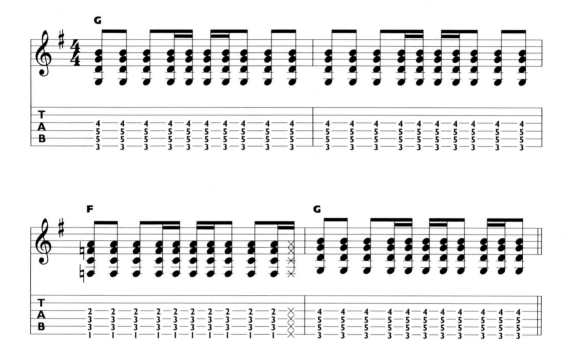

This rhythm features a more contemporary 'skipping' beat feel, in the style
of **Oasis** et al — use up and down strums throughout.

There is no need to stick religiously to the same pattern for more than a bar
at a time, though it could be argued that you are trying to produce a repetitive
'hypnotic' feel, if inspiration deserts you in
the heat of the moment!

'Highwayman on the Gallows'

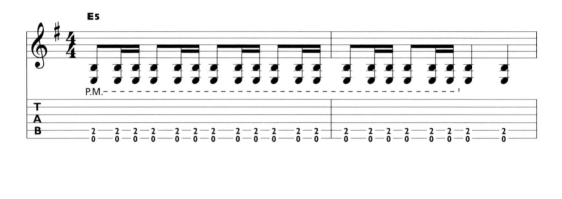

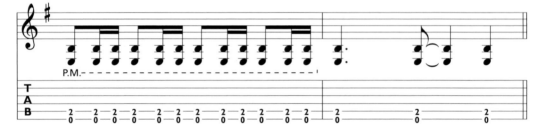

This 'galloping' rhythm has been used on many **Iron Maiden** songs, giving a driving feel, like you're really 'leaning on the beat'.

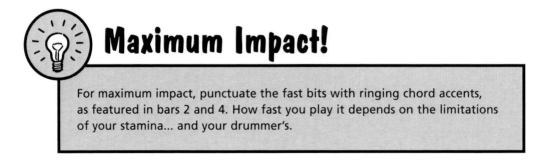

Maximum Impact!

For maximum impact, punctuate the fast bits with ringing chord accents, as featured in bars 2 and 4. How fast you play it depends on the limitations of your stamina... and your drummer's.

'Smells Like Kurt'

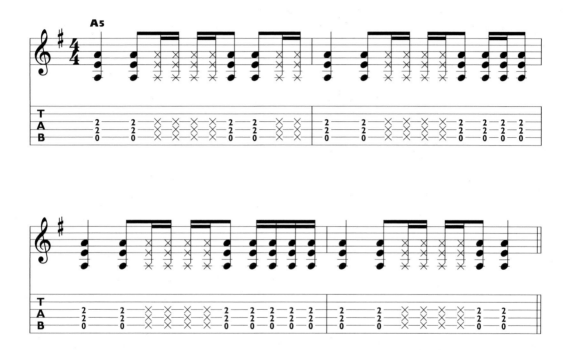

Based round a loose '**Nirvana**' style rhythm feel, this example features a large amount of percussive muted strumming. This keeps the rhythm moving nicely as well as giving you extra time to make your 'seamless' chord changes.

As a general rule, keep these strums from ringing or you will lose the feeling of contrast.

'Angus Gets It On'

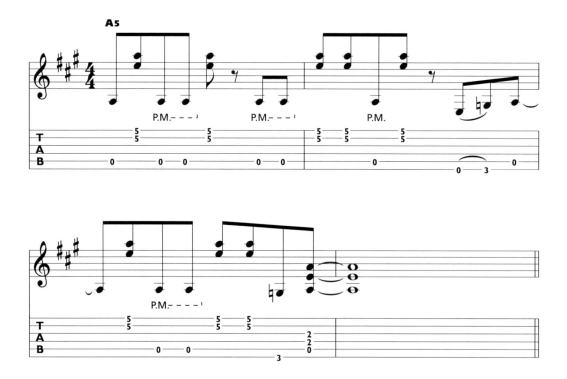

This syncopated, funky rock rhythm in the style of **Marc Bolan** mixes up muted bass rhythms with staccato chord stabs. Bars 2 and 3 both begin with an anticipation (known as an 'anacrusis' to classical players, and as a 'push' to rock rehearsal room dudes).

This A5 chord voicing is a great favourite with AC/DC'S **Angus Young**.

'Spotlight Grabber'

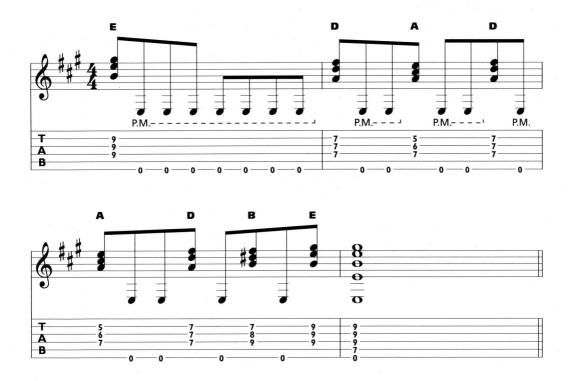

If the worst happens, and you end up chugging along underneath a keyboard player's cheesy chord stabs, get back in the spotlight by duplicating those voicings on the guitar.

This has two advantages; firstly, the bass player only needs to learn one note, and secondly, you can argue that if you've already got the part covered, why don't you just take center stage alone?

'Cult Following'

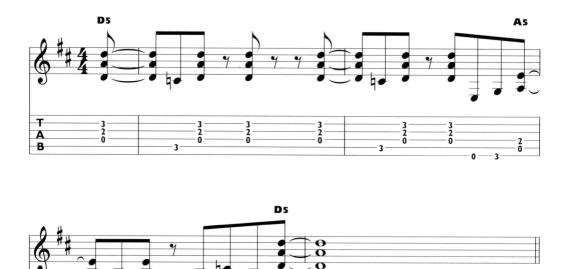

This staccato style calls to mind **Billy Duffy** from The Cult, making as much use of space as it does punchy power chords.

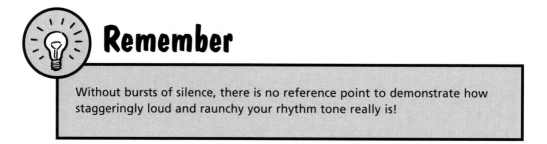

Remember

Without bursts of silence, there is no reference point to demonstrate how staggeringly loud and raunchy your rhythm tone really is!

'Since You Lost Your Eyesight'

Take a big pot of **Rainbow**'s 'Since You've Been Gone' and sprinkle in a little of **Queen**'s 'One Vision', and you'll instantly get a taste for this riff. (Obviously, if you're dealing with a more modern metal situation, quote the names **Pantera**, **Metallica**, **Korn** etc, who do exactly the same thing but with the gain turned up higher!).

For maximum effect, try to make sure the silence between chord stabs is unbroken by string noise or feedback. Onlookers' gasps of awe, however, are perfectly acceptable.

Keith 'The Human Riff' Richards — most Rolling Stones tracks would be unlistenable without his guitar part.

Rock Riffs or 'Play it over and over until it sounds good'

Rock wouldn't have got anywhere without the guitar riff.
Try to imagine 'Smells Like Teen Spirit' without those 'dum-dum,
k'chung chung...' chords at the beginning, or 'A Design For Life'
without the picky bits before the vocal comes in. And the strange
thing about most riffs is — they're so simple, you can't believe
you didn't write them yourself.

What's a riff?

A riff is a short guitar phrase, almost always one, two or four
bars in length, which repeats at various points throughout the track.
It can be transposed (moving into different fingerboard positions
when the chords change) or it may be slightly modified to take
account of the changes.

In this section, we've also included rock 'licks'. A lick is a lead guitar part that
you learn beforehand, and then include as part of a so-called 'improvised' solo.
It follows that licks are, of course, vital to a bluffer's defensive equipment, because
they can be inserted in a lead part without anyone knowing that you prepared
them before the gig.

JARGON

The difference between a riff and a lick is basically that
you may only use a lick once (pretending it's a great phrase you
just thought up) but you can use a riff over and over (demonstrating how
you can make one simple idea into a whole musical experience).

In this section you'll find riffs and licks of varying levels of difficulty, together with
tips and suggestions about when — and when not — to use them. If you're a
complete beginner on guitar, don't be afraid to concentrate purely on the easy
examples — some of them sound more difficult than they actually are.

'Chuck Van Gallagher'

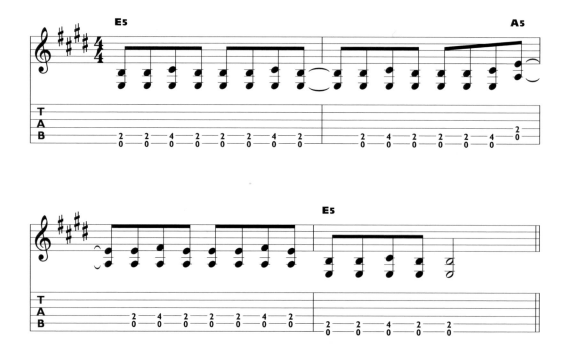

From **Chuck Berry** to **Van Halen** to **Oasis**, this riff has a long history. It's suitable for a wide range of dynamic purposes, so try it ringing wide open or palm muted with accents. This approach will also work in the keys of A and D, without any fingering alterations.

'Arriving Early'

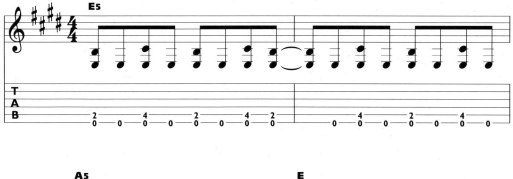

Here's a similar idea, using a more varied picking hand approach.

Check out the anticipations of the following beat before the barline — this gives a little more rhythmic movement and stops the backup from becoming too 'straight'. Including the occasional full E chord adds another dimension and gives a further range of dynamics to choose from.

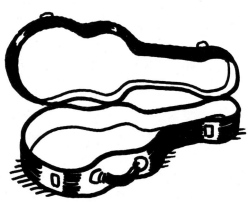

'Who Said Rock Was Difficult?'

This is an easy riff, but play it with your back to a wall of Marshalls and rock deity status is yours for the taking. Using the open position E minor pentatonic scale (see page 75), this riff passes through the chords of E5, A5, and B5, changing the content and style slightly for each.

Play the same riff in a fretting position (without the open strings) and use the opportunity to add loads of taste-free vibrato!

'Mauve Haze'

Taken from the **Hendrix**/late 60s school of rock rhythm playing, this kind of riff, though never out of style, is currently enjoying a resurgence of mainstream popularity.

To avoid unwanted notes sounding from the open E chord, try lightly holding down an E major shape, preventing the fifth, fourth, and third strings from sounding. A semicircular side-to-side movement of the head is optional, but recommended.

'Ritchie's A Smoker'

This **Ritchie Blackmore**-style riff uses diads in the key of G minor (his favorite key).

Mixing open and fretted sounds, there are some dramatic sounding changes; e.g. the Db5 chord, which is reminiscent of **Black Sabbath**, but also hints at more recent material by bands like **Metallica** and **Pantera**.

'You Are Feeling Sleepy...'

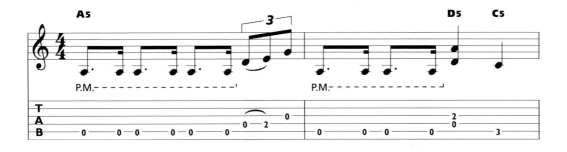

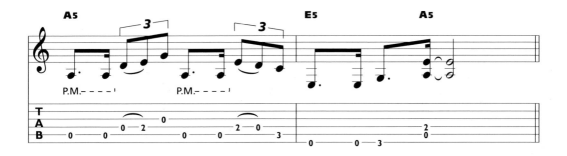

With its pulsing, progressive rock feel, this example would benefit from fairly light palm muting, rather than the super-heavy Punk or Metal style.

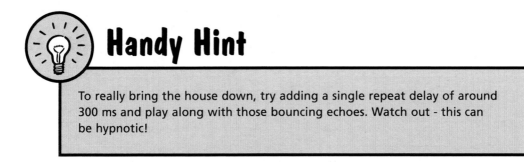

Handy Hint

To really bring the house down, try adding a single repeat delay of around 300 ms and play along with those bouncing echoes. Watch out - this can be hypnotic!

'Machine Gun Metal'

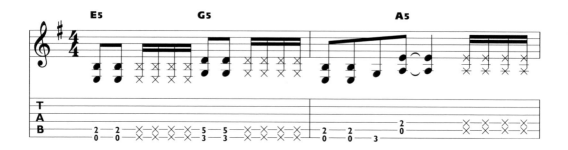

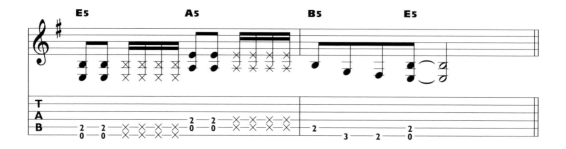

Dial in a really dirty distorted sound and tell the crowd to stand back before you launch into this riff.

The string noise is every bit as important as the chord accents, so don't let your muting hand relax until exactly the right moment. Because the left hand part is fairly easy, you should be able to get this up to a high enough speed to convince other players that you are not to be messed with.

'Leading Astray'

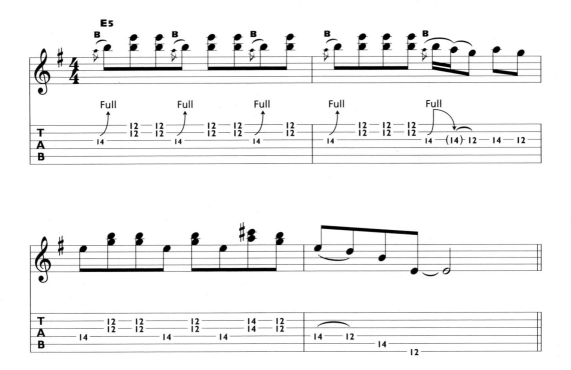

Moving into outright 'lead' territory, this authoritative, attention-grabbing phrase will have everyone hanging on your every note throughout your solo!

The 'double-stop' approach is also very useful if you have a lot of musical space to fill e.g. with a 'power trio' (just bass and drums backing you up). Don't forget to name-check **Chuck Berry** if anyone asks...

'Lonely at the Top'

Whether you're practicing alone, jamming at a soundcheck, or showing off in a music shop (more details about this on page 84), some sort of 'self accompaniment' can make sure your soloing skills can be appreciated even without a band.

Use open strings as bass notes between phrases to imply a backing track. A good bluffer can keep this sort of thing going for 15 minutes or more. **And remember, it doesn't matter if the band's bored, as long as the audience thinks you're cool...**

'Jimmy's Hammer'

Conjuring up images of **Jimmy Page** and **Led Zeppelin**, this hammering riff uses a dual approach of filling every space with frenetic activity, then laying back on some rhythmic spacing and ringing power chords.

Try to play the phrase in bars I and 3 as cleanly as possible — even cutting back on the distortion if necessary. This will make it easier for all to hear just how heavy your playing can be.

'Lizzie's in the Pink'

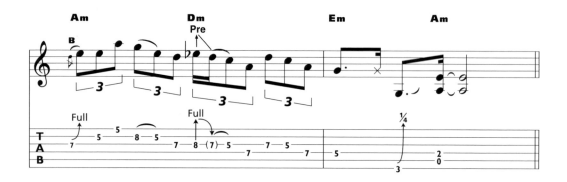

This riff crosses over between lead and rhythm techniques, beginning with a **Thin Lizzy**-style groove which segues into a descending pentatonic phrase.

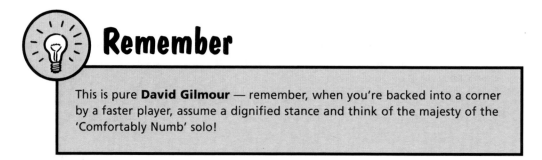 # Remember

This is pure **David Gilmour** — remember, when you're backed into a corner by a faster player, assume a dignified stance and think of the majesty of the 'Comfortably Numb' solo!

'Sprint This Way'

A tricky-sounding bluesy rock pentatonic lick - think of **Aerosmith**'s 'Walk This Way' on steroids! Don't rush this one or the intricacy will be lost on the listener. Rehearse slowly in private, then dash it off carelessly in public.

Try playing this one up at the 12th fret and then using the notes to make up a classy-sounding solo.

'Emergency Speed Lick in G'

Every now and then, we all run out of ideas during a solo. Keep this one on hand if you ever get stuck when you're jamming in G.

Played at a high enough speed, it should dispel any doubts about your natural soloing ability. Even at a steadier pace, the hammer-ons and pull-offs in bar 2 give a degree of fluency that is hard to beat, especially when you nail the pull-off at the end of bar 3.

Use your little finger for this, just before jumping over with the first finger for the concluding hammer-on.

'Superhuman Picking'

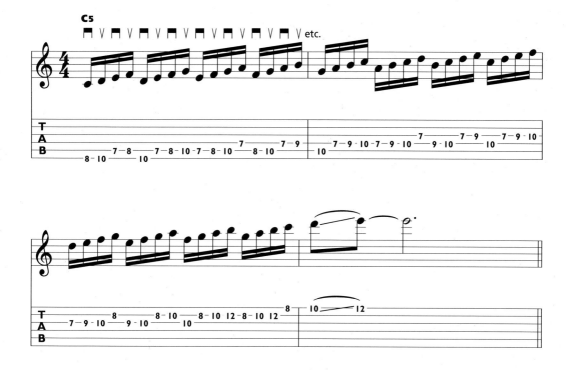

When you need one of those impressive, long alternate picked runs that seems to go on forever, this is just the sort of thing to play.

As with most fast playing, a large proportion of its content is repetition, so it's not nearly as tough as it first appears. Work slowly through the phrase, choosing a comfortable and logical fingering, building up the speed gradually. **Then, rip it up!**

'Sounds Good — Looks Better!'

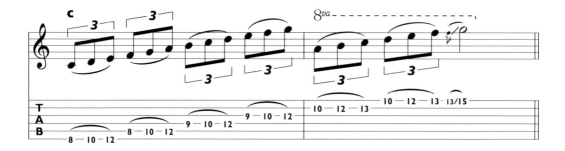

Using three-note-per-string hammer-ons is a great way of adding 'flash' to your solos.

This example also incorporates some position shifts: I've never understood why, but audiences always seem to think you're a better player if they see your hand move along the neck a bit. Once your fingers have learned the shapes, playing this at speed is relatively easy.

Just remember to be ready with a blistering pentatonic phrase to follow it up!

Led Zeppelin were responsible for some of the greatest rock riffs of all time.

'Tapping Without Taste — lick 1'

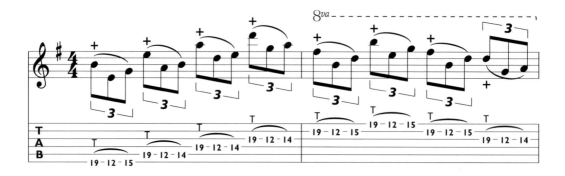

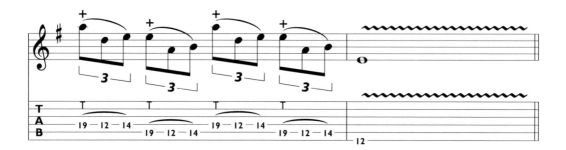

A cascade of arpeggiated patterns will emerge from your guitar when you run through this deceptively simple tapping sequence.

Looking closely, you will see that the fretting hand part is none other than the simple E minor pentatonic scale. The tapping hand part is even easier, staying at the 19th fret throughout. **Trust me — it's hard to get a bad sound from this lick.**

'Tapping Without Taste — lick 2'

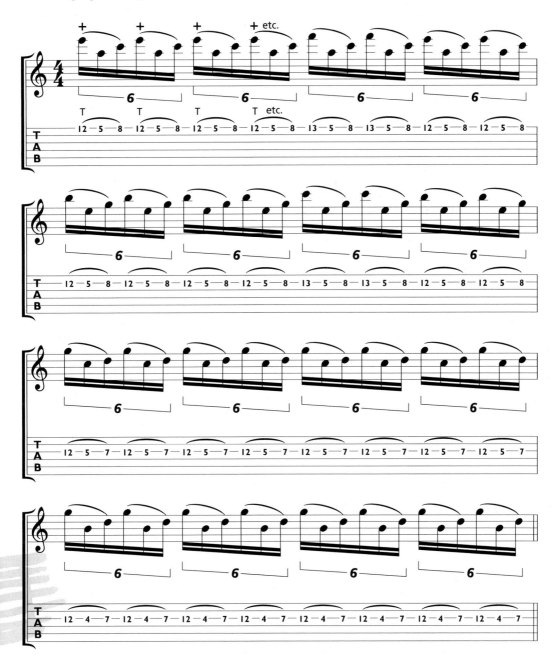

Tapping frenzy ahoy! This classical-sounding pattern is reminiscent of **Eddie Van Halen** and **Randy Rhoads**. In this case, the tapping finger is moved to provide a shifting melody at the top line, which changes slightly as the line moves across the strings. **Steve Vai** and **Joe Satriani** have taken this technique to even further extremes, based on the same blueprint.

'Sweep Picking Made Easy(ish)'

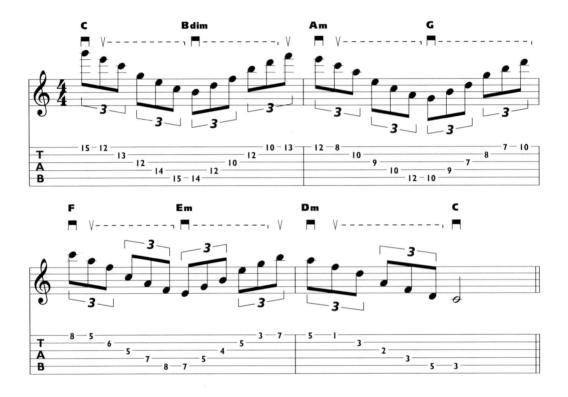

Sooner or later any conversation between rock guitarists comes round to sweep picking, so it's worth knowing at least a couple of shapes. Here's how you do it: pick one note, then pick across the strings *all in the same direction*, fretting each note as you play. As soon as a note has sounded (and as you pick the next one), slightly release pressure on it so the whole thing doesn't blur into a strummed chord.

Tip

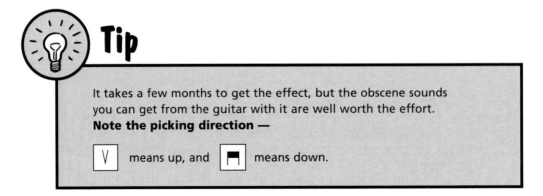

It takes a few months to get the effect, but the obscene sounds you can get from the guitar with it are well worth the effort.
Note the picking direction —

V   means up, and ⊓   means down.

'Abuse at the Bar'

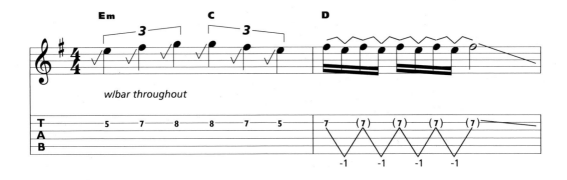

w/bar throughout

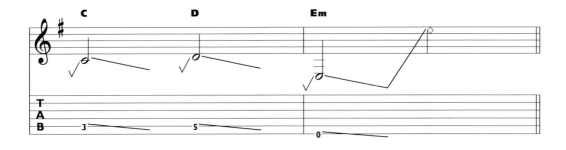

An essential part of the rock guitarist's equipment during the mid/late '80s was a locking tremolo, engineered to take all manner of abuse without going out of tune.

It's all extremely addictive once you start, so here is one example featuring a few tricks. In the last bar, touch a fifth fret harmonic on the sixth string, while it is slack, then let it raise back up to pitch.

Many players learn **Satriani** licks by heart and pass them off as their own.

'Outrageous!'

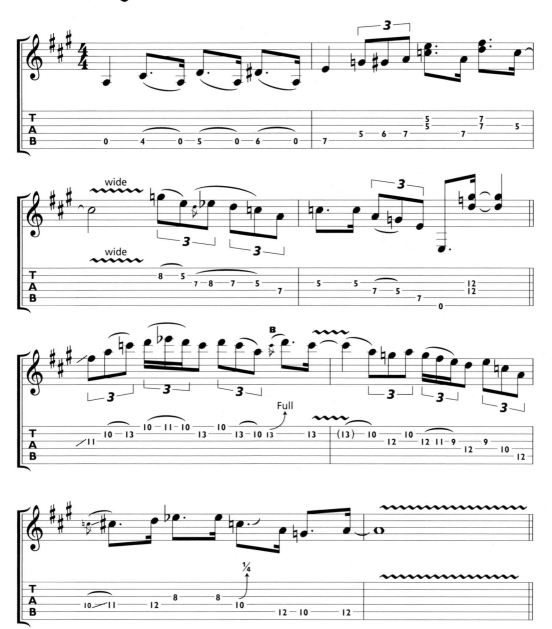

And to finish this section, here is a longer more difficult phrase, giving you a little more room to demonstrate some of the tricks/phrases in context. Make sure you choose the most convenient and comfortable fingering pattern for each of the phrases — start with the premise of 'a finger per fret' and modify it from there. Perhaps the overall feel can be compared to **Ritchie Blackmore** circa 1970, or **Joe Satriani**'s 'Satch Boogie'.

Chord Sequences or 'Can't I just slide the same bar chord up and down?'

Rock players are notoriously lazy when it comes to learning chord sequences — they think of the rhythm backing as the 'boring bit' that gets in the way of the solos. Also, many only learn one bar shape for each chord (because, in true faking style, this will help you get by in most situations!).

In this section you'll find a few simple two- and three-chord sequences which you can use in a variety of rock styles.

Power Chords

The rock bluffer's friend

Power chords, or '5 chords' as they're sometimes known, are the most essential rhythm weapon in the rocking rhythmist's arsenal. They contain only two notes per octave, leaving out the major or minor third (so if a chord of C major, or C, contains notes of C, E and G, a chord of C5 will contain only C and G). They have two great advantages — one, they sound better (i.e. more powerful!) through distortion or overdrive; and two, they're usually easier to play. Shown in the fretboxes are four examples of common power chord shapes — these are in the key of A but can be moved to any fret. Learn 'em!

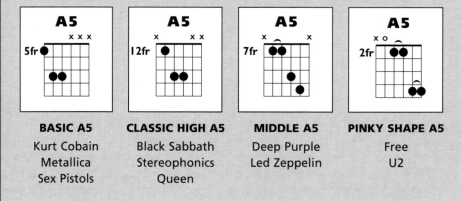

BASIC A5	CLASSIC HIGH A5	MIDDLE A5	PINKY SHAPE A5
Kurt Cobain	Black Sabbath	Deep Purple	Free
Metallica	Stereophonics	Led Zeppelin	U2
Sex Pistols	Queen		

'Room to Flaunt It'

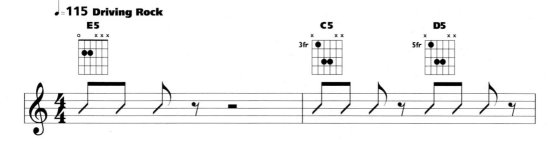

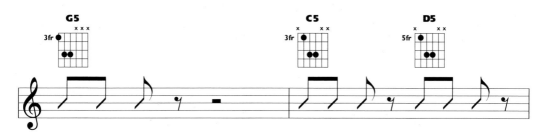

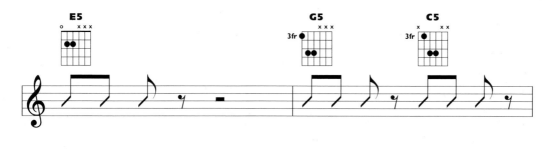

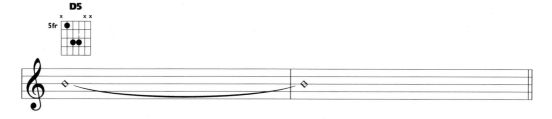

A typical driving rock sequence, with characteristic gaps punctuating bars 1, 3, and 5. Any ideas based around the E minor Pentatonic, blues scale, or minor scale will fit with no problems. Try to persuade your bass player and drummer to keep quiet during the gaps, so your hard-learned lead licks are certain to be heard without anything clouding the picture.

'Maximum Potential'

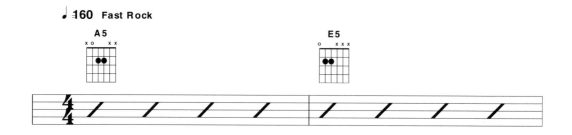

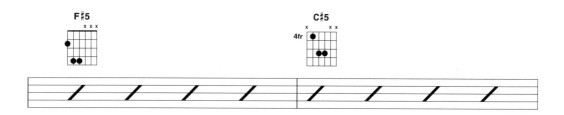

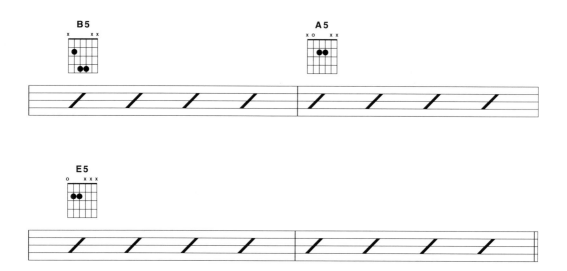

This is notated as a straight four to the bar, but should be played using a few of the rhythm patterns you've already tried. For soloing, the F#m pentatonic or blues scale will fit anywhere, with all the usual bends available. The reason for choosing this key is that it allows maximum choice of cool rock licks at all times.

'Classical Era'

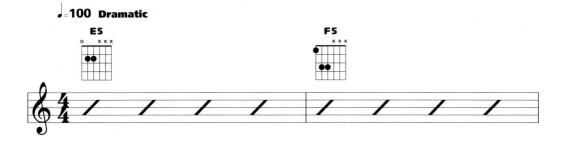

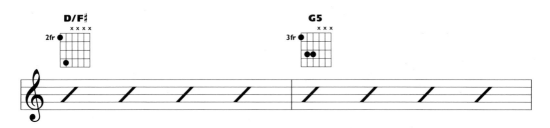

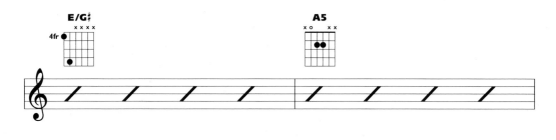

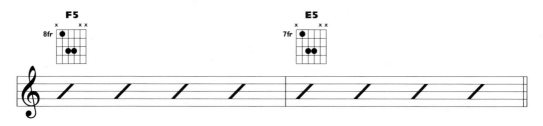

Ascending in a dramatic and menacing manner, it's time to rise to the challenge
with a couple of neo-classical flourishes. Tapping is always good in a situation like
this, but another option could be the 'eastern' sounding harmonic minor scale.
In this case it would work best over the suspended, or 'slash' chords — you can,
of course, mix it up with the ever-present A blues scale!

'Hearing Voices'

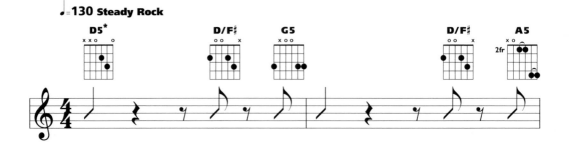

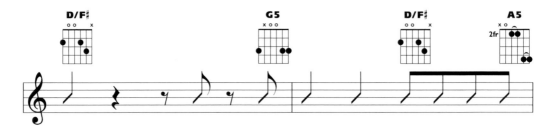

This one's straight out of **AC/DC**'s 'Very Small Book of Rhythm Patterns'. Sometimes the 'voicing' of a chord — as these alternative versions show — can make them really stand out as something very different from the standard versions. If you're soloing, try the B blues or pentatonic scale, along with the A Mixolydian mode.

'Jackson Five'

♩=140 **Driving Rock**

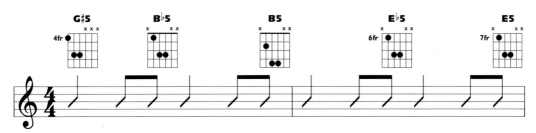

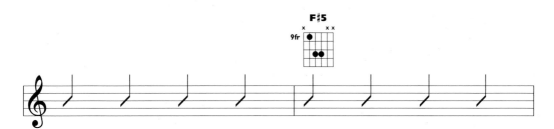

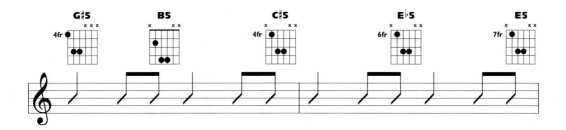

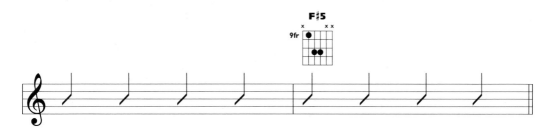

Most rock music features '5' chords — also known as '**power chords**'. These consist of root and fifth only, meaning they're neither major nor minor. This, of course, makes them indispensable to the rock bluffer, because you can get away with a whole bunch of scale choices without the audience hearing any wrong notes. This example, in the key of G♯, would work best with G♯m pentatonic, G♯ Dorian mode, or G♯ blues scale.

Scales or
'It may not sound too good —
but look how fast I can play it...'

A great deal of nonsense is talked about scales by guitarists, so it's usually possible to fool the assembled company with very little knowledge. Ask any reasonably experienced player to perform the major scale, or any of the modes, and nine times out of ten they'll zip up and down the fingerboard at high speed. Ask the same player to take a solo, and they'll go back to the same simple blues licks they've been playing for years.

So it's a sure bet that you'll produce gasps of awe just for creating a solo out of these scales. The ones featured here are the most foolproof — it's difficult to put a wrong foot forward with some of them — and will be more than enough to take you through 95% of the soloing situations that the average rock track puts you in.

Scales Tip

You'll also have the added advantage of being able to devise nonchalant phrases such as "I just take a simple natural minor pattern and modalize it via the Dorian and Mixolydian with a couple of basic position shifts. Kids' stuff, really, but I guess it works." And if you get a smack in the face, they're just jealous...

All scale fretboxes are shown upright, with the headstock at the top, and the strings ascending in pitch from left to right: i.e. **the lowest E string is on the left.**

A box around a note or open string simply means that note is a 'root' note. I.e. **in E minor any boxed out notes will be E.**

E Minor Pentatonic - the foolproof scale

To start with, everyone needs to know this 'industry standard' scale. All of the great rock soloists have used this kind of scale shape at one time or another. The infinite possibilities are probably easiest to explore when playing over power chords, but you'll find you can use these notes over many sequences in the key of E or E minor.

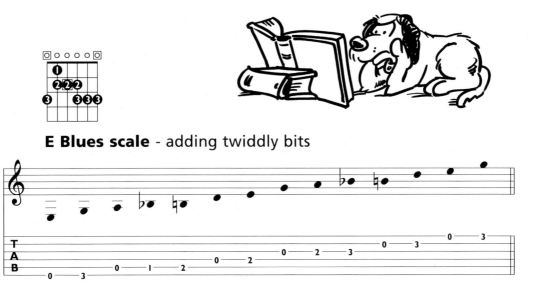

E Blues scale - adding twiddly bits

Moving on slightly from the standard pentatonic shape, adding a 'flatted fifth' (in this case B♭) gives you a whole new range of licks to play with. The ♭5 is generally considered to be a 'passing note' i.e. don't let it ring too long, or it will sound as if you're playing off key. If this should happen, claim that you are 'exploring the use of suspense in a harmonic context'.

A Minor Pentatonic - the rocker's friend

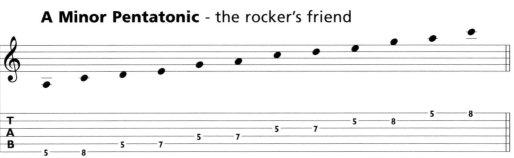

Moving the first position E minor pentatonic to an all-fretted position gives this fingering pattern. This example is in the key of A, but it's moveable to all keys just by starting at a different fret. Try bending the note at the 7th fret, third string — **you can almost hear some of those 'Stairway to Heaven' licks.**

A Blues scale - more twiddles

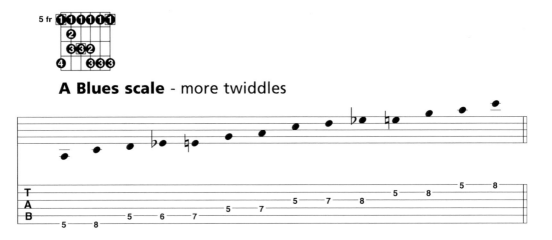

Adding a ♭5 (in the key of A, this would be E♭) demonstrates the same added amount of flexibility as it does in E. It might seem strange that adding just one note (and a rather unfriendly-sounding one at that) can open up so many possibilities, but without it, rock solos the world over would sound even more samey than they already do!

A natural minor - spoiled for choice

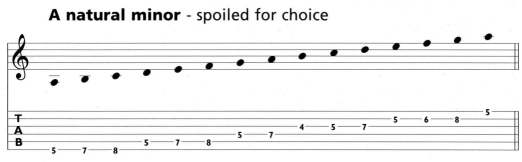

Keyboard players don't understand this one, because they don't do it in their grade 1 exam! However, next to the minor pentatonic and blues scales, it's one of the most useful for 'sensitive' rock solos. If the backing chords are basically minor, this scale works great for those 'big ballad' moments of the set.

A Mixolydian mode - wizardry and wands

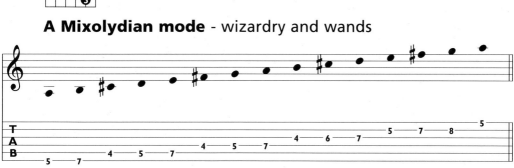

Some say **Jimmy Page** and **Kula Shaker** wouldn't have had a career without this scale, and it does work well over 'mystic' drone notes, but it's actually much more versatile than that. Try this scale whenever the main backing chord is a 7th (in this case, A7) — it works especially well on R&B, rock 'n' roll, and some jazz/rock tracks. Theoretically, it's just a normal major scale with the 7th note flatted, but you should always refer to it by its modal name to command maximum appreciation of your 'years' of rock study.

A Dorian mode - spinning in space

Due to the fact that modal theory is often taught fairly badly, many guitarists think of this exclusively as a 'D minor' mode, but like any scale, it can be played in every key. Think of it as a natural minor scale, but with the sixth note raised by one fret. Dorian phrases can work well to add interest to a straightforward minor pentatonic solo. Its 'spacious' sound can be heard in tracks by **The Eagles, Pink Floyd, Satriani,** and **Santana**.

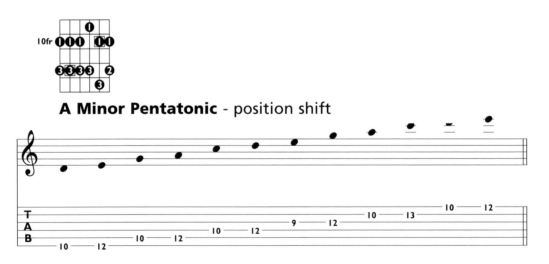

A Minor Pentatonic - position shift

This alternative position of A minor pentatonic starts at the tenth fret of the sixth string. This pattern offers a slightly different take on the same licks you've tried with the 'basic' shape. As the notes fall on different strings, there are a few surprises as to what will and will not work using hammer-ons and string bends. This is a very easy shape to use, but you'll be amazed how many guitar players never bother to learn it.

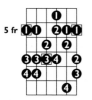

A Harmonic Minor - Full of Eastern Promise

Using this scale instantly gives the impression that you are classically trained. If you play it throughout a solo, it starts sounding a bit 'Eastern', so if that's not the effect you want, then just use it over the fifth chord (i.e. if you're in A minor, play A harmonic minor when there's an E or E7 in the backing).

A Minor Pentatonic - position shift 2

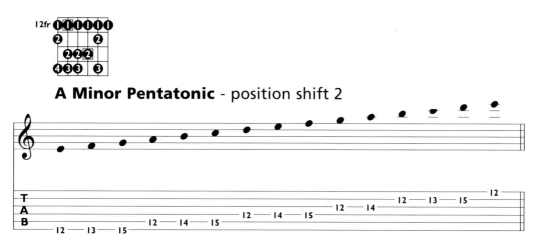

The rock player can never learn too many minor pentatonic shapes, and this one is great for single-note melodies with plenty of bent notes. Because the first finger is always anchored at the 12th fret, there are some awesome hammer-ons and pull-offs available with very little effort.

Music Shop Classic or 'How do I fit everything in this book into 24 bars of showing off?'

This custom-designed showpiece should amaze any onlookers and cynical staff at your local guitar shop. It's been specially devised to be utterly without the shackles of musical subtlety, emotional validity or artistic good taste.

First of all, be sure to play it at a tempo which enables you to make all the position shifts evenly — it's far better to nail a lick perfectly at a slower tempo than make a mess of it at high speed (unless you're playing *very* fast, that is, in which case any old rubbish will do).

There are a few tricks in here to help you out, too. It uses lots of open bass notes to aid fast position shifts.

The **Led Zep**-meets **Aerosmith** riff section should wake up the staff and draw a crowd (which usually takes 11-12 bars or so), then when everyone's watching, the flashy single-note solo licks can become more frequent.

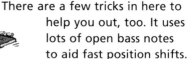

Warning

At no point should you show undue strain, so make sure you're so well-practiced that you can play it without breaking into a sweat. That way, everyone in the shop will be secretly imagining what you could do if you were *really* trying.

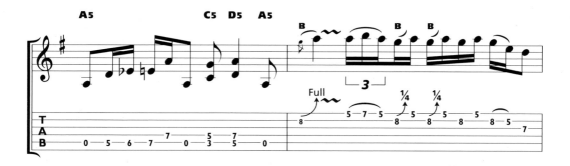

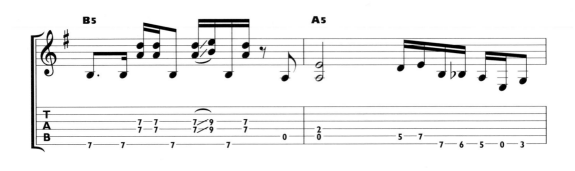

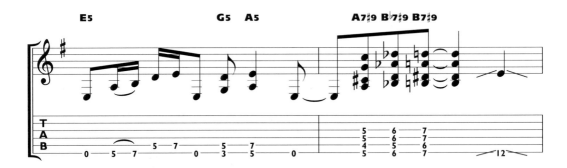

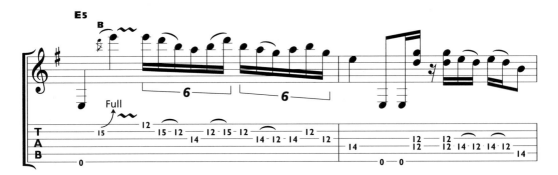

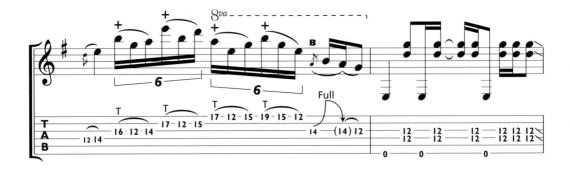

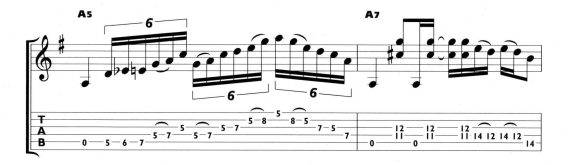

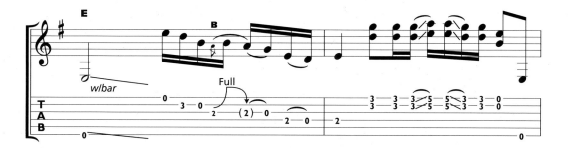

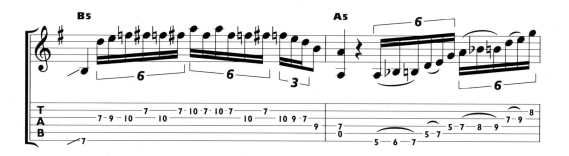

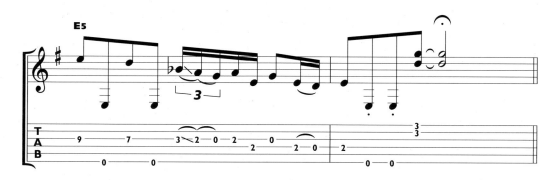

Music Shop Riffs — the dos and don'ts

If you *have* to play well-known riffs in a music shop, you might as well choose one of the best. On this page, I've listed the top 20 rock riffs currently being played in music shops.

You can get away with some of them yourself — indeed, several are expected of you — but others will result in banishment to cliché hell. Next to each riff is listed an advisability rating (10 means it's essential repertoire, 1 means you'll be lucky to leave the shop with your nose still attached to your face) and tips on which bit to play.

Title	Artist	Advisability rating	Tips
Stairway to Heaven	Led Zeppelin	0	One of only two intros to be banned absolutely by international treaty. Never, EVER play this song.
Smoke on the Water	Deep Purple	1	And this is the other one. Tip — most people start it on two open strings — it's actually a double-stop at the 5th fret. Point this out to others, but DO NOT play it yourself.
Smells Like Teen Spirit	Nirvana	4	Intro chord riff. Quite useful for the basic player who wants to sound authentic, but should only be played a maximum of twice through.
Enter Sandman	Metallica	7	Intro picking. Over 10 years old and still going strong.
Every Breath You Take	The Police	5	A bit worn, this one. Message in a Bottle is more difficult but worth the effort.
Design for Life	Manic Street Preachers	7	Recorded in 1996, and still very popular. C major 7, 3rd fret. Dead easy. Make sure you stop before the difficult E♭ bit.
All Right Now	Free	1/8	Intro — if you can play it *exactly* like the original, then go for it, otherwise steer well clear.

Title	Artist	Advisability rating	Tips
Layla	Eric Clapton	2	Without a big backing, this one always sounds weak played solo. Avoid.
Eruption	Van Halen	6	A bit passé now, but still pretty impressive if you put in the work to learn it all the way through.
Ain't Talkin' Bout Love	Van Halen	8	Rejuvenated by Apollo 440's sampled version, this one wins extra points.
Purple Haze	Jimi Hendrix	3	Main riff. You might get away with it if you've got just the right fuzz sound.
Sultans of Swing	Dire Straits	2	Intro chord/lead part. OK for clean sounds, but difficult if you're a plectrum player. Insist on a compressor pedal.
Wonderwall	Oasis	1	Between 1995 and 1998, this evil beast stalked the music shop community like an... awful chord riff. The only consolation is that it's played on acoustic.
Back In Black	AC/DC	4	Main chord/lead riff. AC/DC will always be in these charts, but *please* make sure the guitar's in tune before you start.
Paranoid	Black Sabbath	3	1-bar intro. And don't play any more than that.
Sweet Home Alabama	Lynyrd Skynyrd	6	Chord intro. Everybody knows it, but no-one can quite remember what it is. Easy to play if you know D, C, and G.
Whole Lotta Love	Led Zeppelin	9	Main riff. Possibly rock's most famous guitar line, known equally for the original as for its status as the Top of the Pops theme.
Parisienne Walkways	Gary Moore	6	Main melody. Lots of people play this, but few play it well. Only to be attempted if your string bends are accurate.
Hotel California	The Eagles	5	Well-known, but not as clichéd as 'Stairway...'. Acoustic players should go for the fingerstyle intro. Electric players try the pull-off arpeggios at the end.
Blackbird	The Beatles	6	Whole song. A good one if you're new to fingerstyle, but only to be attempted if you can play it all the way through. Yes, even the middle part!

Amps or
'The foolproof guide to guitar tone'

Hopefully by now you should know that the most important things in rock music are visual. Having a guitar with a Fender logo is, in the eyes of players, better than one with a Squier logo. When Oasis released their first album, many people thought that they sounded like the Beatles — primarily because Noel was seen in a John Lennon-style hat. And, of course, two Marshall stacks look twice as good as one.

However, some will try to convince you that the most important thing about a guitar is its tone. And to know about tone, you need to know about amps. In days gone by, an amp was designed to reproduce the guitar sound as cleanly as possible. Not any more. These days having the right amp is as important as... well, having the right color plectrum.

Opening a valve

You'll be told throughout that valve or 'tube' amps are preferable to transistor or 'solid-state' models, and even though many people who say this wouldn't have a clue in a blindfold test, you can't call yourself a rock guitar player unless you take a stance on the issue of valves.

Generally, it's safer to take the tube option — firstly, most of the pro players do choose valve amps, so you're in safe company, and secondly, it's easier to defend old technology by describing it as 'classic' and 'legendary' than to attempt to praise current items because they're 'small' or 'reliable'. Think of your amp as a car — would you rather be seen in a 1960s Mustang or a brand new Hyundai?

The mighty Marshall stack. Sounds great, but you wouldn't want to take it on the bus.

Tone Tips

10 tips for the ultimate Rock guitar tone

1. Use the right guitar! Les Paul-type or other humbucking pickup for fat, thick rock tones, Strat-type for bluesy biting sounds. You won't get satisfying rock sounds out of a Strat. Unless you're **Jimi Hendrix**. Or **Carlos Santana**. Or **The Edge**. But apart from those guys, it's impossible to get a decent rock tone out of a Strat. Oh, yeah, and there's **Ritchie Blackmore** too.

2. Use the right pickup! Neck pickup is great for warm, middly leads, but the rest of the time, if you really want pounding rhythm parts and squealing lead, the bridge pickup is the one to choose. Tone control all the way up, please!

3. Remember, the more distortion you use, the more difficult it is to hear what's going on. This can totally destroy a rhythm guitar part...

4. ...however, if you're playing single-note lead, a really high gain setting can improve sustain, create fantastic harmonics, and make your guitar sound more expensive than it really is.

5. If you use a compressor, put it *before* the distortion in the effects chain to avoid microphonic feedback. If you value your eardrums, that is.

6. To smooth out your lead sound, add a delay of about 200-400ms to the distorted tone, and mix it between 20% and 50% of the main signal. This turns any solo from a sputtering moped in a pothole to a Ferrari being driven on a frozen lake. By Sean Connery.

7. Rock lead parts can sometimes be improved by boosting the midrange a bit...

8. ...and rhythm parts by cutting some mid from the sound.

9. You can get away with a dreadful guitar tone if your vibrato's good...

10. ...and vice versa.

Guitars! or 'Surely it's more important to be a good player?'

More important than your technique, amp tone, even hairstyle, is the type of guitar you're seen with. A player can get away with horrendous musicianship if they own an instrument to die for. The reasoning goes something like this; if you see someone with a guitar which cost more than your house, you get to thinking that they wouldn't have spent all that money unless they could really get the best out of it.

All too often, of course, it just means that they've got more cash than you. But admit it, for a second, when you saw that guitar in its case, you thought the owner was a better player than you, didn't you?

Mouth open and RAWWK!

Here, then, is a selection of the guitars to own if you want to command maximum respect among the rock community. All usage of jargon has, of course, been maximized for your convenience.

Gibson Les Paul

DATA:
First introduced in 1952 ('Gold Top' model).
Designed by the eponymous guitarist.
Humbuckers replaced single-coil pickups in
1957. Various off-shoots (Les Paul Junior, Les Paul Special, Les Paul
Deluxe etc) but the two best-known are the Standard and Custom.

FAMOUS NAMES:
Gary Moore, Jimmy Page, Joe Perry, Slash, Ace Frehley, and Mike
Bloomfield.

DESIGN:
Solid body (originally mahogany) with arched top,
two humbucking pickups with three-way selector
switch. Two volume, two tone controls.

SOUND:
Les Paul wanted the guitar to have a 20-second sustain (hence the
mahogany), and this is the instrument's most famous characteristic.
Combination of solid construction and high-output pickups makes
it suitable for high-gain, long distorted sounds (hence the rock-blues
leanings of the above-named players). Typical adjectives include
'singing', 'ringing', 'stinging', 'swinging' (jazzers only), 'gunslinging'
(guitar heroes only).

KNOWLEDGEABLE FACT:
Some 'Les Pauls' have double cutaways and a flat top — these
are referred to as 'SG-style'. Generally, though, the name Les
Paul is used by players to describe the arch-top, single-cutaway
guitar shown in the photo.

INSTANT OPINION:
Just say any old rubbish involving
sustain, e.g. **"the sustain on my old
LP, it's incredible, but that's 'cos I
got mine from a guy who knew
the milkman who used to deliver
to Clapton's house back in '64."**

ACCEPTABLE CRITICISM:
Try wearing a solid mahogany guitar on a shoulder strap
throughout a 2-hour gig, then come up with your own...

The 1952 Les Paul Gold Top - ringing, singing, and gunslinging.

Fender Stratocaster

DATA:

First introduced in 1954. Design has hardly
changed since. Some models manufactured
in Japan from early 1980s, under the Squier
brand name. Strats are now made in the following
countries (listed in descending order of price
and quality): USA, Japan, Korea, Mexico, and China. Technically,
its low-output pickups and high frets shouldn't make it a rock machine,
but plenty of players have put in the effort and got results.

FAMOUS NAMES:

Jimi Hendrix, Ritchie Blackmore, Jeff Beck, Eric Clapton, George
Harrison, David Gilmour.

DESIGN:

3 single-coil pickups, double-cutaway, solid body.
Floating bridge vibrato unit (though for serious
whammy-bar madness you'll need a locking unit).

SOUND:

Generally brighter than other rock guitars, due to its single-coil pickups.
Adjectives to use include 'sparkling', 'glassy', 'sharp', 'honking', 'bell-like',
'squealing', 'crisp'...

KNOWLEDGEABLE FACT:

Single-ply scratchplates were replaced by three-ply
white/black/white versions in 1959. Impress other Strat
users by noting that their single-ply scratchplate (very
common on copies) is "based on the classic '57 design".

INSTANT OPINION:

"Early '80s Japanese Squiers were actually better made
than the American Strats at the time." (true in some cases,
and vague enough to convince everyone with your
confident use of such a sweeping statement).

ACCEPTABLE CRITICISM:

Cheaper copies are often prone
to microphonic feedback, and
most Strats will give you
mains hum unless you get
replacement pickups.

!!?#

This is a 1959 model, but then you knew that by looking at the scratchplate, didn't you?

Fender Telecaster

DATA:
First introduced in 1948 as the 'Broadcaster' but this was changed because the Gretsch company made a drumkit of the same name. Various options were available later, including humbucking pickups, semi-solid body and even a paisley finish, but the basic Tele we now know and love is almost exactly the same as it was 50 years ago.

FAMOUS NAMES:
Keith Richards, Chrissie Hynde, Graham Coxon, Danny Gatton, The Hellecasters.

DESIGN:
2 single-coil pickups, 3-way switch, one volume, one tone. No tremolo block. No complex switching options. No fancy contours. A Tele is basically a plank with strings on it.

SOUND:
A little fatter than a Strat, but not as rounded in tone as a Les Paul. Used through the right amp/pedal, the bridge pickup can create a rich 'growling' sound that no other guitar can imitate. Adjectives include 'cutting', 'gutsy' and 'biting'. You get the idea.

KNOWLEDGEABLE FACT:
There's a Fender guitar called an Esquire which is basically a Tele with bridge pickup only (it's cheaper, and most rock players rarely use the neck pickup anyway). But for some reason, people still prefer the Tele...

INSTANT OPINION:
"It's a solid, functional piece of equipment, like a Sten gun..." (Keith Richards).

ACCEPTABLE CRITICISM:
Only 21 frets, so if you want to play cheesy metal nonsense at the top of the neck, you're looking at the wrong guitar...

The Fender Telecaster - a solid, functional plank with strings.

And just in case...

If someone asks you about any
other guitar, it's usually safest to
steer the conversation back to one of the 'big three' by saying
something like: "Yeah, I know what you mean about the Delectrolux
Tri-Tonic Sound-u-Like model, but it can't really replace the warm
tone of a real Les Paul..." However, if you get really stuck, here
are a few bite-size snippets on other rock guitars:

1. Gibson SG

Double-cutaway, twin-humbucking flat top
solid-body. As played by **Frank Zappa**, Black Sabbath's
Tony Iommi and AC/DC's **Angus Young**.

Tiny neck width has been known to annoy big-fingered rock players.

2. Gibson Flying V

Possibly the first deliberately-designed 'rock' guitar, even though
it was introduced long before heavy metal was anything more than
a buzzword for nuclear physicists. Fixed bridge, solid body, twin humbuckers.

Hendrix owned one, but it's also been played by many a metaller, including
Michael Schenker and **J. Geils**. Blues greats **Albert King** and **Lonnie Mack** are
also well-known V players.

3. 'Superstrats'

During the 1980s, the US company Jackson had the bright idea of taking the world's most popular guitar and giving it a turbo-charge. So they whacked a high-output humbucking pickup in the bridge and put a 'locking' tremolo unit in, allowing all sorts of whammy-bar shenanigans at high volume without feedback, mains hum or tuning problems.

You don't see them so much nowadays, but the Superstrat is still one of the most versatile guitars around.

4. DIY guitars

**If you're famous enough,
why not design your own?**
Mind you, if you're that well-known, you've faked your way to the top already, so you won't be needing this book...

Although some players play 'signature' versions of classic designs, others actually have their own models. **Bo Diddley**, **Joe Satriani**, **Steve Vai**, **Randy Rhoads**, **Eddie Van Halen** and **Nuno Bettencourt** all have had guitars made for them by the manufacturers, like this 7-string Ibanez Universe á la Steve Vai.

Rock Lyrics or
'In my day you could hear the words...'

No-one likes writing lyrics. Hey, you didn't get into rock to be a poet — if you had, you'd spend your time wandering round fields of daffodils in a frilly shirt. And even if you do take the trouble to string a few rhymes together, no-one cares what you're singing about, right?

Well, broadly-speaking that's true, and in recent (post-grunge) years, many bands' rock lyrics have perhaps become even less important. However, there are some subjects that you need to cover, and others which you must avoid, if you're going to convince anyone that you're a 'proper' rock songwriter.

What to write about?

Anything which mentions motor vehicles is instant cool. And the less wheels they've got, the heavier the rock. **Chuck Berry**'s 'No Particular Place To Go' was drivin' along in its automobile, but ten years later **Steppenwolf**'s motorcycle anthem 'Born To Be Wild' had its motor runnin' out on the highway.

Meat Loaf's been defying the laws of gravity atop a Harley Davidson for years. But that doesn't mean it's cool to be seen in your grandfather's Gremlin — even with black windows, flames up the sides and **Metallica** blaring out of every window...

Meat Loaf -
two-wheeled
rock

Steppenwolf - born wild

If you're going to write about historical subjects, it needs to be 500 years ago or more. Anything to do with medieval torture, thunder crashing over castle ramparts and maidens being saved from certain death is fine for some types of rock and metal. Just don't mention dragons or you'll be accused of being a **Genesis** fan.

Politics is OK, as long as you don't mind being branded 'alternative rock' (**Rage Against the Machine**, **Skunk Anansie** etc). Keep it contemporary, though. If you start writing about the hangman's noose or 18th century Luddism, that's fine, but keep in mind that these days there's not an awful lot of work for **Jethro Tull** tribute bands.

Rock lyricists have been writing about sex for years, and it's all been done, so don't bother to try and shock anyone. If **Whitesnake** can get away with songs like 'Slide It In' (subtle use of metaphor) and the **Stones** can do 'Brown Sugar' (sexism and racism all in the one track) there's not a lot of point in taking things any further.

Lyrical Genius

> **Generally**, your love story should go — boy meets girl (**verse 1**), boy asks girl for a dance (**verse 2**), they 'rock' all night long (**chorus**), stopping only for a guitar **solo** before we're reminded how they met (**repeat verse 1**).

So our ultimate rock lyric needs to feature a rock dude on a motorbike — wait, let's be really heavy and make it a unicycle — in the year 1500. He's gotta save his girl from the clutches of the evil Zarg (random sci-fi is usually OK too) who lives in a castle in the ancient land of Gandalf (or pick any other word from The Hobbit).

She's exploited by the despotic power of MTV, which is oppressively sapping her sense of political self-determination (might be tricky to make that bit fly), but by the end of the middle eight she meets up with our unicycling hero and they rock the night away. Classic!

Outro

So now you've got it all — the background information, the CD collection, the licks, the techniques, the gear, and the lyrics. Now all you need is a gig, and unfortunately you'll find that without an extremely good demo, many mainstream venues won't have anything to do with an unknown rock band.

The secret, of course, is to fake your way in. Disguise yourself as another type of musician (short hair, sweaty nylon T-shirt and Seattle accent ought to put you firmly in the 'indie' camp) and describe your set as something like 'power-pop for the new generation'. That way, the first time they'll know what you sound like is when the bikes start rolling up outside. And by then it'll be too late...

If you've enjoyed this book, why not check out the other books in this great new series, available from all good music and book retailers, or in case of difficulty, direct from Music Sales (see page 2).

It's Easy to Fake...

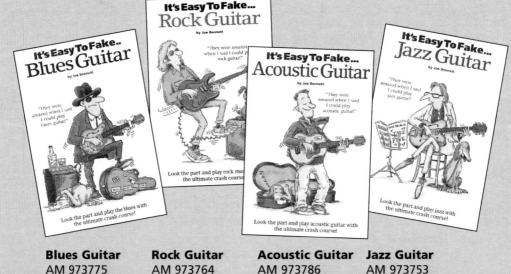

| Blues Guitar | Rock Guitar | Acoustic Guitar | Jazz Guitar |
| AM 973775 | AM 973764 | AM 973786 | AM 973753 |

JOE BENNETT has been teaching guitar for fifteen years, and regularly works as a session guitarist. He is also a senior examiner in electric guitar for The London College of Music and Head of Popular Music at City of Bath College. Joe's publications include the *Guitar: To Go!* and *Really Easy Guitar* series, and *The Little Book of Scales*, plus tracks and articles for *Future Music*, *PowerOn* and *Total Guitar* magazines.